SEEING HITLER

April 30, 1945 - in Nussdorf, Germany
WWII Eyewitness Account of Aubrey M. Temples

The incredible, but absolutely factual, story of a World War II American POW, who gives a face to face, eyewitness account of Adolf Hitler's escape from Germany on the very day he was supposed to have committed suicide in Berlin.

I0085806

Check out an exclusive interview with the author at:

www.aubreytemples.com
www.seeinghitler.com

Also be sure to check out this book recently published by Peter David Orr:

www.eyewitnesstohitlersescape.com

ISBN #978-0-578-43870-2

This is an effort to furnish my family and friends with some facts regarding my time in the military during World War II. No report could be complete, especially one written some fifty years later. Unfortunately, I was not able to record all the dates, times and places because of the circumstance under which I existed most of the time.

Beginning in 1939, Germany, with help from Italy, marched through country after country in Europe. Young men in America were drafted starting in 1940. On December 7, 1941, the Japanese bombed Pearl Harbor. On December 8 war was declared on Japan, Germany and Italy. It was no surprise, since most of the news was about the war in Europe. It was news by radio, since this was well before television.

England and France had declared war on Germany and Italy, but neither of them had enough military strength to deter them, especially Germany. Under the leadership of Adolph Hitler, Germany had the greatest military force in the world at that time.

Most of the young men in this country were very conscientious and joined some branch of the service. I was 17 years old and thought I should be a pilot in the Air Corps. I had never ridden in a plane, but it seemed the most glamorous of all the military service.

At that time, if you could pass a written test, as well as the physical, you could become a pilot in training. I went to an induction station, passed both the test and physical. They were about to swear me in when a Sergeant informed them I had not taken the color test. They gave me one; I flunked and was not sworn in. I tried a second induction station; they operated by the same rules. The Navy was no better; they didn't like color-blind people either!

Sometime later I went with a busload of draftees to the Tyler, TX, induction station and found the army was not so particular and they accepted me. Sarah Gross and I were married on May 30, 1942, and I was not inducted until November 1, 1943.

Off to Camp Walters, Mineral Wells, Texas, for a few days; then on a troop train for a ride to Camp Wheeler, Georgia, located outside Macon. After four months of training, we were declared competent soldiers and were off to war.

Each man was given a fifteen day delay in route to visit family before going overseas. My family had grown. We had a two week old baby, Rebecca Jane. A short stay at home, then on to Fort Meade, Maryland. More shots and off to Camp Miles

Standish, Massachusetts. A few days later we boarded a train and rode to Boston Harbor to board the Susan B. Anthony, the largest passenger ship of the U.S. Navy. We were docked at Pier 16. We joined a convoy of ships of many descriptions. The trip over was uneventful. We landed at Glasgow, Scotland. This was a beautiful harbor with multicolored flowers on a long sloping hillside. The houses had many colored tile roofs.

A British General came aboard to welcome us. I quickly found that he spoke English and we spoke American. It was very difficult to understand him. We remained on ship for another night. We were so far north it didn't get dark in the evening. Some of the fellows played cards all night on deck.

We boarded a train and rode through Scotland, England, and to an American Army Camp in Wales. We met and talked to the English people. They talked funny and everyone rode bicycles. One elderly man proudly told us he had been to London one time, though it was only 75 miles away.

We were issued rifles, clothing and equipment. About a week later, seventeen of the several thousand were selected to go to the 82nd Airborne Division stationed at Leicester, England. We were informed that we would be trained as Glider Pilots. I had not seen a glider and being color blind, I wondered if I could qualify. Our first training was to ride in an American glider. These gliders were made of aluminum tubing covered with material that looked like ducking with a coat of paint. Skids, much like snowmobiles, were used for landing and take-off. Approximately twenty men could ride in the glider along with extra equipment. Our glider was pulled by a C-47, a two engine cargo plane. A nylon rope some 100 yards long was attached to the plane and glider. We rode for several minutes and returned to the airport. The gliders were made for one way trips.

Next we rode in a British Horsa glider, which is two or three times the size of the American Glider. This glider was made of plywood and had a landing gear much like airplanes. After a few minutes we came back for a landing. I expected to use the runway, but the pilot came in on the grass. The pilot held the nose up for a while; finally the landing area of the glider hit the grass, caught, and turned over. No one was hurt, although we tumbled around inside. The pilot knew, but we were unaware, that the landing gear had fallen off.

A few weeks later we were informed that a large number of air corps pilots were failing their flight instructions, but had sufficient training to be glider pilots. No one ever mentioned my being color blind. We were assigned to the 82nd Airborne Division as regular paratrooper replacements.

I think it was early August, 1944, when General Eisenhower came and talked to our division. He mentioned many things that had been done, but other things must also be done. He did not tell us then, but we were scheduled to jump in Holland in September, 1944. We were also assigned to the British Second Army.

A Second Lieutenant was sent to the Air Corps Base to make arrangements for sleeping and eating. The General at the Air Corps Base did not think it would rain, so the cots were set outside along with temporary kitchens for cooking. It rained all night; we left wet and without breakfast.

Our Company's objective was to destroy a German ammunition

dump just outside the small town of Mook, Holland. After jumping from a plane on September 17, 1944 and hitting the ground, we formed lines on each side of a narrow road and walked the two miles or more to the town. Some women and girls came by and offered us some milk and cookies. A few could speak English and told us how happy they were to be liberated. We didn't stop.

Someone at the front of the line dropped his gas mask and everyone else dropped their gas mask on the stack. They were large and difficult to carry. I wondered if I might need the gas mask later.

When we reached Mook, population 200 - 300 by my estimate, every building was destroyed or badly damaged. We didn't see anyone or anything except a small pig in a pen that looked like a chicken coop. We found and destroyed the ammunition dump by firing into it so that it destroyed itself.

Dead cattle were lying around bloated and smelling. Soon we met the Germans and the war was on again. We were able to gain ground every day. At night we sent small groups to check the strength and location of the enemy. This was very dangerous. If you were discovered, you were shot or shot at. I had two bullets go through my trouser leg.

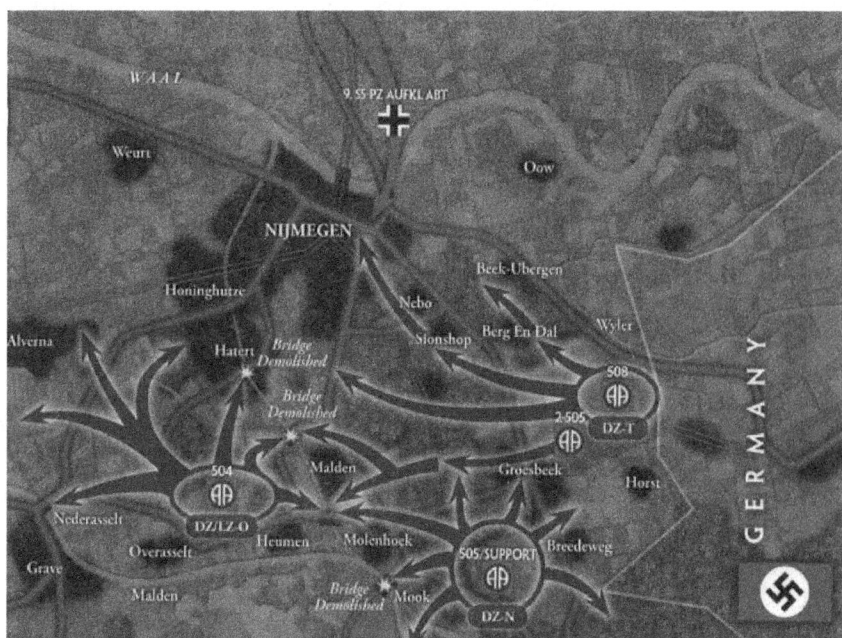

After about a week on the front lines, another company came to replace us for a day. They didn't arrive until 3:00 p.m. We walked a mile or two behind the lines to a beautiful park-like area with large pine trees scattered around. We were close enough to hear the sounds of war.

We were eating field rations, so no food was cooked. There was a fine mist in the air and it turned dark early. Everyone had lost a lot of sleep, so we tried to get to sleep early. Shortly after 8:00 p.m. we heard large incoming shells. We had never heard any shells so large, so we figured they were from a railroad gun. They first began to hit 300 to 400 yards away. Gradually they landed closer and closer. We were in our foxholes. Quickly the shells were hitting the large pine trees and shrapnel was hitting everything.

Orders were given to move out; it was as dark as midnight, no light except when the shells exploded. We ran into trees, foxholes and each other, but finally got everyone out. Some were wounded, but none were killed. We walked down a narrow road. The shelling stopped as soon as we left the area. This led us to believe someone close by was directing the shots.

On the trip down the narrow road I could feel something warm running down my right side. I felt on myself and didn't find any wound. We found an area to spend the night in another wooded area. I decided to get a drink out of my canteen and found the top had been completely removed by shrapnel. It was the warm water running down my side I had felt as I walked. The next morning I borrowed a canteen from a soldier who had been killed. Before noon we had relieved the group that had relieved us. It was a very short day of rest.

Not long after we were back in place, we could hear an American calling for help. It appeared he was very near the German line. He was asking for medics and a stretcher. Two German medics came out carrying a white flag and a stretcher. When they arrived, the wounded American continued to call for American medics. Two Americans with their white flag and stretcher came out and carried him to the American line. By this time both German and American troops were in "No Man's Land" without weapons.

A few Americans could speak German and many Germans could speak at least some English. I talked with a young German soldier. He was married and had a child. He was 21 years old and had been in the service for six years, four years in combat areas. He showed me pictures of his wife and child and wished he could go home. For thirty to forty-five minutes we had an unauthorized truce. Then came orders from both sides to return to their places. I thought that war was not the answer to the misunderstandings made by governmental leaders. Again we started shooting at the soldiers we had befriended.

Every day the British came over with their Lancaster bombers and dropped supplies. Every day they landed behind the German lines even though we had proper markers. We thought the Germans must have known how to mark the area for drops.

Almost daily we took prisoners. A good part of them walked in with their hands in the air. On October 2, 1944, we marched forward several miles. After dark we advanced another three or four miles, crossing wooded areas, open pasture land, farm land and finally across a sugar beet field that ended at a blacktop road. Orders were given to "dig-in", which means to dig a hole for protection. I suggested to the Company Commander that we move back some distance because there was a thick row of trees across the road. He didn't think it necessary, but I noted that he did return 100 yards or more to the rear. Our foxhole was not more than 15 to 20 feet from the road. We heard nothing and saw no one, but there were many German soldiers across the road.

The next morning when someone raised their head, a German shot at us. We could talk to our buddies in the next hole, so we could send word back and forth. We were scheduled to move back when it became dark. A few minutes before dark we could hear tanks moving around. By looking over the edge of our hole, we could see a tank about 175 to 200 yards away sitting by a house. Our bazooka man had only one shell; he raised, fired and missed. He did hit the house which was soon blazing brightly. In fact, it was light enough to read a paper. We didn't think it was the best time to leave our foxhole.

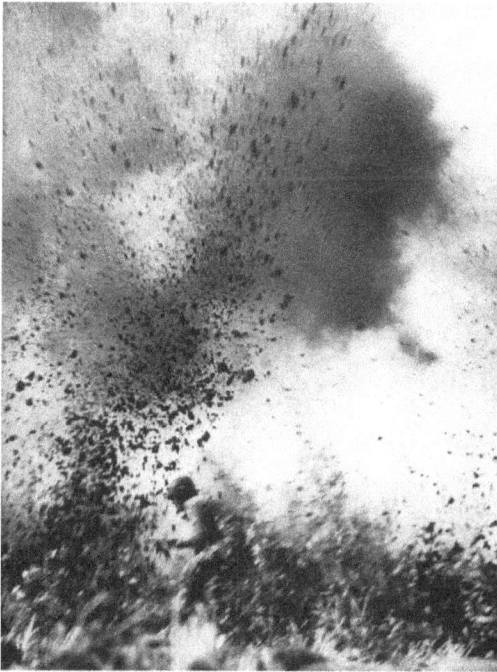

A terrible explosion happened in the foxhole of John Martin and me. I was unconscious for some time. When I aroused, I knew it must have been a hand grenade. I felt around to see if I had been hit, but didn't feel any injuries. I asked John if he was hurt; he didn't answer, so he was probably unconscious. I heard a tank, looked over the edge of the foxhole and saw a large tank coming my way from 50 to 60 feet away. I had time for a quick prayer and ducked my head.

Sometime later I felt someone digging me out and saw it was German soldiers. I was taken out of the foxhole first, and realized I had broken bones, because when I moved I could feel them rubbing against each other. When John was taken out, his right leg was almost removed from his body. They placed him on a stretcher and I gave him a shot of morphine. One of the German medics told me that John would get good care in the hospital. Here I was a prisoner-of-war; something I had not considered. I had thought of being killed or being wounded. No other live American was there, and I wondered if the Army would know what happened. I also wondered if my wife and family would be notified.

I was led into a nearby house that the Germans used as headquarters. I was searched, but nothing was taken except military equipment. They examined my back and agreed it was badly hurt, but no medical treatment was available. I found that my left hand, particularly in the thumb area, was badly cut. I wonder why I didn't feel the cut when I was giving myself the self-examination.

Four or five of the Germans could speak English and discussed with each other, as well as with me, how we could have lived through the hand grenade and the tank, especially in the soft sandy soil. One talked at length about how fortunate I was to be alive. They also promised that the medical staff in a prison camp would properly repair my damage.

I don't remember checking my watch to determine how long I may have been unconscious. Soon everyone went outside where six or seven dead German soldiers were being placed like cordwood in the pickup. The first four or five bodies were stiff and easy to load; the last two were not stiff and were very difficult to load. I felt sure they were the ones I had shot and

I wondered and hoped the Germans didn't think I was the one who had shot them. I saw the pickup was made by Chevrolet, and after looking closer, saw it was a 1938 car that had been altered to make a pickup. The lights were on and only a small slit allowed light to come through. A guard, carrying a rifle, motioned for me to climb up and set on the cab facing toward the back. He got on the other side of the cab and kept his rifle continually pointed at me. Driving down the road, it was almost as if there were no lights. We crossed a long bridge and I assumed we were in Germany.

They drove to a German army camp with tents similar to those we had in England. An officer was found who spoke English and knew quite a bit about the 82nd Division. He asked many questions, I gave him only my name, rank and serial number. When I didn't cooperate, he began to yell, scream and threaten me. After thirty minutes or so he quietly told the driver to go on.

Some miles further the truck stopped at a crossroad. The guard motioned for me to get off of the truck. I took a long step off the truck and realized how sore I was. I didn't have any pain when they dug me out of the foxhole. The guard and I walked down the road heading south. The moon was shining and was very bright, I thought he might take me somewhere and shoot me. After a few hundred yards, I saw a real castle, large, with moat, drawbridge and a hallway wide enough to drive a truck through. Soldiers were working as if it were daytime, and it was now well past midnight. Two soldiers went with us to a large room, which had no furniture except a long ladder lying on the floor. The two new German soldiers lifted the ladder to an opening in the ceiling about twenty feet high. The guard pointed up, so I climbed and found a dim light and five American prisoners, all from the 82nd Division. Each had heard the ladder and checked to see who was coming. They were asleep in a few minutes.

"No bedding was furnished; we slept on a wooden floor. By now my back was hurting, even though it didn't hurt when I was taken out of the foxhole.

The others woke early and we discussed the interrogation. Each agreed to tell nothing. I recall wishing I still had my morphine so I could give myself a shot. When we climbed down, the interrogation started one on one. They tried to secure information by threatening, yelling, screaming, and intimation.

About mid-morning, they put all of us in one room and tried to pit one against the other. No one gave any information. At noontime all the German military people ate. Lunch was brought on a tray to those doing the interrogation and the guards. They ate, we watched. We were lined up outside the castle and a photographer took our pictures, and then took movie pictures for quite a while. More questions were asked. We didn't respond. They said some soldiers would come and we would stand before the firing squad. Eight or ten soldiers did come with rifles. On command they aimed the rifles at us and removed the safety. I looked at each gun and it seemed all were pointing at me. This was a stand-off for thirty minutes or so, aiming; then standing with the rifle beside them, but they never fired.

At about 4:00 p.m. an ugly loaf of bread was laid on the table. The loaf was not wrapped, we saw several people handle it. Finally someone got a kitchen knife, cut the loaf in six pieces, one for each of us. This was my first prisoner-of-war food. After this, we were allowed to return to our castle suite, via the ladder. My back seemed to hurt worse each day. I found I could lie on my back, not move and get some sleep.

One of the other Americans prisoners told us he had been captured by the Germans during the D-Day invasion. He was moved from place to place, finally to a warehouse type building in Paris. Several windowpanes were missing from the building and some Frenchman came in with glass and ladders for the repairs. After finishing their task, our fellow prisoner said he asked for clothes so he could escape. He had been raised in

France until he was a teenager, when his family decided to move to the States. His grandmother and other relatives still lived in Paris. One of the window workers was wearing two suits of clothes, so he let our friend have one. He walked out carrying a ladder, visited with his grandmother, worked his way to the coast, got a ride to England and rejoined his old outfit. His Company Commander thought he had stayed in France to visit his family, not believing he was actually captured by the Germans. A soldier is not allowed to fight again in the same theater of war after he has been a prisoner, but his commander sent him back where he was captured a second time.

When it was apparent that he would be captured again, he destroyed his dog tag, identification of all types and took a new name and serial number. He did not want the Germans to know he had escaped from them in France. He also informed us how we would be treated, food we would get and what to expect. He told us all our possessions would be taken from us. I cut a slit in the lining of my Eisenhower jacket and tucked my watch, knife and Bible (New Testament).

The following morning we went down for more interrogation. Before noon two guards took us, by foot, some three or four miles to a warehouse-type building where another twenty-five or thirty Americans were being held. Among this group were about twenty who had been on one glider that was shot down in German held territory. They surrendered, along with their captain.

That day we ate something that looked like cookies but weren't sweet. They were not good, but then we were hungry. At about dark a group of Polish farm workers came with a couple of instruments to play and sing for us.

It seems the locks were not good on the building we were occupying, so we were ordered to move a few hundred yards away. This building would lock, but had cobblestone blocks for a floor. No beds or furniture were available, but I did get a board about a foot wide and four feet long. My back felt better on the board than the cobblestone floor.

The following day, eight or ten guards arrived on two flatbed Ford trucks. We were loaded and drove for an hour or longer and arrived at a large prisoner-of-war camp in Limburg. Here we were searched, as our French speaking friend had said we would be. Some who objected were locked in a fenced area with no water or food. When they were ready to drink or eat, they could tell the guard. The guard took their possessions and turned the water on from a faucet, which was in the enclosure. Afterwards, they joined the other prisoners.

An American Master Sergeant had been captured long before I was captured. He spoke German fluently and had changed his loyalty from America to Germany. He had at least two uniforms, both cleaned and pressed and his shoes shined. He had the appearance of a real soldier.

He was the contact for the Germans and was abusive, both in language and force, if necessary. He had German guards to back up his actions. He apparently had plenty of food, not just the allotment for prisoners-of-war. After the war, he was court-martialed and given many years in prison.

We quickly learned the meaning of food, as dictated by the Germans. For breakfast, nothing; at lunch, a bowl of thin soup with a few cabbage leaves floating around. It really looked like dishwater. Our big meal was dinner when we were given a small boiled potato without salt, pepper or seasoning, and a slice of the awful black bread. We didn't know all the contents of the bread, but could see quite a lot of sawdust. We had seen some loaves of bread on the battlefields, which had been left by the Germans. We could smell the bread and after a rain, it would pop open like popcorn. I found out after the war that the bread was made from 50% bruised rye grain, 20% sliced sugar beets, 20% tree flour (sawdust) and 10% minced leaves and straw.

We slept on bunks made like a box with thin straw mattresses. The bunk was slightly better than the hard boards. I requested medical treatment and was told no service was available until I reached a permanent camp.

We were assigned work details on a regular basis. Most work details were to clean rubble from damaged buildings, or repair streets where bombs had hit. My back was terribly sore and I could hardly move around. The guards were aware I couldn't work and would let me sit or stand around.

Sometime prior to World War II, the Ford Motor Company had built a plant to build trucks, which was located in Limburg. The trucks used by the Germans had the Ford insignia exactly like those in the United States. The Germans had attempted to camouflage the plant by constructing the streets over the building. The intent was to prevent the enemy aircraft from dropping bombs on the plant.

On one detail, I was standing around and a young woman came up with a sack of potatoes, possibly 20 to 25 pounds. She asked the guard to have someone carry the potatoes to the third floor. He pointed at me, so I took the potatoes in my right arm and proceeded up the stairs. When I returned, I heard someone calling "hello". Looking up, the lady with the potatoes was dropping a small paper sack. I caught it, and there was a piece of cake inside. She spoke to the guard, apparently telling him the cake was for me.

A few days later we were told that we would go to a permanent camp that afternoon. After 3:00 p.m., we boarded a railroad car, the type used to haul freight. It was not very large, approximately one-half the size of American railroad cars. Eighty of us were aboard. When we boarded the railroad car, a can of food was given to every two men. The can had a hole punched in it to prevent the storing of food for an escape try. I had not met the fellow who was to share my can, but we stayed together. After waiting an hour or more, we decided to eat the food. The can was the size of a small soup can. The food tasted good, looked like dog food, but wasn't much for two men.

About dark the train began to move. My back was so sore I could feel every jerk and jolt of the train. After a couple of hours, the train stopped and we sat still for what seemed like hours. We were told before leaving that we would be in the new camp for breakfast. There were so many men on board that we couldn't all lie down at one time. We worked out a schedule for one-third to sleep, one-third to sit and one-third to stand. I took my turn the same as everyone else, because each position seemed to hurt as bad as the other.

Fresh air was a problem, especially when we were sitting still. There were two small round windows in the car, one near the front on one side, the other near the rear on the other side.

The Germans didn't seem to forget anything. A can, about five gallon size, was placed inside to serve as the restroom. We didn't move much the next day, only a short distance forward and back. However, they did forget to supply water for drinking. The second night the train moved forward and back. One time, when we were parked, the air raid alarm sounded. We stayed locked on the train. Bombs fell about 100 yards away. Some shrapnel hit the car, but none of the men were hurt.

The second day was much like the first. We asked for water, but none was forthcoming. The third morning we received water; everyone was terribly thirsty. The water revived us as much as a meal. Before noon we arrived at Moosberg, about fifteen miles from Munich. There was a large prison camp, Stalag VII A. The three days traveling in the railroad car had proved to be the most difficult of my life.

The camp had probably 100 buildings with double barbed wire fencing and rolled barbed wire in between. Also guard towers were along the perimeter. Each building had a separate fence. We were ushered into a building approximately forty feet by eighty feet. There were fifteen bunks built to accommodate twelve men. They were three high, two wide and two long. We slept in box-type beds about six inches deep by six and one-half feet long and thirty inches wide. Each bed had a thin straw mattress. The remaining furniture was a table, approximately three feet by five feet, and a coal burning stove vented through the ceiling. There was a water faucet outside the door and a pit toilet by the back fence.

I chose a top bunk, climbed in, and right above my head was written, "Kilroy Was Here", a message seen everywhere during the war. I found that the straw mattress was thin enough to feel the boards, but it was still better in comparison to the train. We had not had food in more than two days and received none until the regular feeding time at noon. We were then served the familiar bowl of soup with floating cabbage leaves, nothing more.

I requested medical treatment and was told to report to the medical unit the following morning. I was in line early, but a large number of men were there well before I arrived. The medical unit consisted of two men, two chairs, a large box for a table, a few bottles of medicine and a few boxes of tape. When my time arrived, I spoke to a medical helper of some kind. The doctor was French and didn't speak English. The helper examined my back, and after some painful time, he told me a shoulder blade and three ribs were broken. He spoke to the doctor in French, the doctor kept working on another patient. The helper retrieved some paper tape, about two inches wide, and wrapped it around my body from my waist to armpits. The doctor kept repeating the same word that I thought was "tighter". He did a pretty neat job. I could then move without pain. I went to another line to see the doctor about my hand that had been cut with shrapnel. My hand appeared as if it might rot off. Before my turn, another soldier with a little finger badly damaged was having something done. The doctor, through the interrupter, told the man to turn his head. When he looked again, his finger had been removed and some powder and bandage had been applied. For me, he picked up a scalpel. I looked at my hand and told him I would go back to the barracks and let the Lord heal it. After some time, it did heal, and I never went back to the medical unit.

Starting the following day, we had work details. We would ride a train to Munich in box cars, like the boxcar used on our long trip, and usually clear rubble from bomb damaged buildings, repair streets damaged by bombs, or sometimes repair railroad tracks that had been bombed.

Because we rode in the freight cars, we would arrive in the railroad yard. The switches were hand operated and had a metal handle about three feet high. In order to change tracks, the handle had to be moved forward or backward. When walking across the railroad yard, we would go on either side of the switch and change its direction. Apparently, it didn't do much good because I never saw trains hit each other.

The most difficult task was removing bodies from buildings that had been bombed. Usually civilians helped with this task. My back was sore for a while after we arrived at the new camp. I would show the guards the tape on my ribs and didn't have to work.

It was uncommon to have a work detail on Sunday. I can only remember one or two. After my back had healed sufficiently to work, three of us went on a work detail one Sunday morning. A guard and a driver went along also. When we arrived at the truck to be used, I noted it had a device that looked like a thirty gallon hot water heater attached to the right back of the engine. It had a fire box at the bottom where the driver was starting a fire with small pieces of wood. Somehow the heat caused a gas to be produced that would serve as a gasoline substitute. The motor did not start easily, nor did it run well after starting. We traveled a few miles before the driver stopped to rekindle the fire. Once we were going again, we reached our destination, a railroad car on a siding. Other railroad cars were put in the prison proper, but this railroad car was not. The driver opened the boxcar and backed up to the door.

The car was loaded with boxes approximately 6" x 14" x 20", which had two metal bands around each box. Some printing was on the boxes, but we couldn't read it. We starting unloading and in a very short time had the truck loaded and one-half or more of the railroad car empty. The driver left by himself and the guard stayed with us. Apples had fallen from some trees and he invited us to eat all we wanted. It was our meal for the day.

When the truck returned, we began loading again. Soon we could see one box that was open near the back of the car, by a round window. We didn't say anything to the guards and worked around the open box. When we reached the open box, we saw that the two metal bands had been cut; three loaves of cheese were still there and evidence to indicate three loaves were missing. The person who took the cheese had also broken the window (about 8" in diameter) and cut his hand while getting in. He left blood stains on top of the boxes nearby. I put two loaves of cheese in my paratrooper pockets and suggested that one of the other fellows take the last one. Both of the prisoners were afraid to take it. I told them it was a perfect crime, evidence pointed to someone else. I even told them they were already prisoners, what else could the Germans do.

Finally I called the guard inside, showed him the damage. He apparently didn't suspect us, but got some older man from the railroad company to come and complete a form. This took forty-five minutes to an hour to accomplish. At last we finished loading, and the guard asked us to get more apples. He gestured as how to put them in our pockets. My pockets were already full of cheese.

When we reached the main gate, the truck stopped before entering the prison. The first man in line was searched, but they let him keep his apples. The guard who had been with us for the day called to the guards at the gate, apparently saying he had authorized this. I went second and wasn't searched. The third prisoner was searched, but he also got to keep his apples. Once we were safely inside, the two fellows said, "Where is our cheese?" I divided the cheese with everyone and soon it was gone.

When we first arrived at Stalag VII A, some British prisoners were acting as barrack leaders. They soon left and we were to elect someone to represent us and speak for everyone. The election was held by the raising of hands, and we elected a barrack leader. It was me. Apparently, because I had devised the system of standing, sitting and lying on the railroad car, I was the only one nominated.

Each morning we lined up and were counted by the guards.

Our first instruction in speaking the German language was to learn to count, as well as some profanity. We picked up other words, but found it hard to speak properly.

On one work detail we were sent to a Catholic organization of some kind. We saw only Nuns; one acted as our boss. We reworked some flower beds, filled in some holes where bombs had hit, but didn't work hard. At noon the Nun, who was our boss, took all of us, as well as the guards, to a public restaurant. She ordered a bowl of soup, a large bowl with vegetables and meat. I recall she told the waitress to serve the prisoners, then the guards, and finally herself.

One day as we were walking down a main street in Munich a guard looked up at a tall building and said, "Glockenspiel, glockenspiel". We looked up and could see some statues, but didn't realize it was rather famous.

When we first arrived in Munich, it was a beautiful city with some damage around the railroad station. Flowers were growing in flower boxes on every building and house. There were many small parks with flowers, as well as many small plots where someone had planted flowers. The windows were clean, the streets and sidewalks immaculate, not even a cigarette butt. Nothing needed paint, even in war time.

Our Radio

When you have 180 Americans together, you have talent for almost any task. One fellow informed me he could build a radio if people would bring him parts from the work areas. I informed the other men and the next day the first parts were brought in. Our radio-man found a piece of wood about ten inches wide and three feet long. He used wire to tie these parts to the board and to each other. Some parts were duplicates, and we had to take them back to the work site to discard them. We found a hiding place for the radio by raising a loose board under one of the bunks.

Within two weeks he had everything he needed, except a speaker. A week or so later someone found a speaker not more than five inches in diameter. He attached the wires and said, "We have a radio". I wasn't so sure. We plugged in the electrical cord and soon were hearing some voices we couldn't understand. By turning the dial we got BBC: London, and heard about fifteen minutes of news. We turned it off and hid it again. At 10:00 p.m. we listened to another fifteen minutes, then put the radio in the hiding place. About 2:00 a.m. some twenty or more German troops from Privates to First Lieutenants were in our barracks with the lights on. They walked to the bunk, had the men get off, moved the bunk, raised the board, and took our radio. They left without speaking to anyone.

I asked five men I felt I could trust to try to identify anyone who was suspicious. One fellow who spoke with an accent said he was from Philadelphia, but others from the area didn't think he knew much about the city or state. His military unit was a small communications group that no one had heard of. He may or may not have been guilty, but we knew he ate the same food as us and slept on the same type bed. He was in our barracks until I went on the farm detail. We did not catch him talking to the guards or leaving notes.

Our Showers

One of the few things we had to look forward to was a shower. We took a shower about once a month. My paper tape was getting hard and breaking apart. I was afraid the tape would come off with water. My back seemed to be alright by now and I wanted to shower more than anything.

We were furnished soap, something on the order of lye soap, but it seemed to work well in the soft water. I would first wash my hair, because we didn't know how long they would leave the water on. We would stay in the shower as long as the water was running.

My paper tape didn't seem to be bothered by the water, I think I enjoyed the shower as much as a good meal.

Official Information

Every ten days or so an English-speaking officer would be in the compound when we lined up for head count. After the count was finished, he would talk to us about the status of the war, German version.

He first talked about the Americans and the English. He said several times that they were losing their foothold in France and would soon be ineffective. He didn't mention the bombers coming over almost daily and the devastation we saw in Munich on the work details. Each time he discussed how the Russians were retreating and were no threat to the German people.

We considered it strange that when American or British bombers came over, we were required to go inside during the daylight hours. If the plane came over at night, all electric power was turned off. Immediately afterwards, lights would come on, approximately two miles to the Southwest. We thought that possibly a factory was being protected.

On one daylight raid, everyone had been warned to go inside. It must have been Sunday; otherwise we would have been at work. One fellow in the barracks across from us was cooking something in his little Russian-made cooker. The guard called to him several times and fired a shot at him. He seemed to ignore everything. Finally the guard shot him, and he was carried off on a stretcher. I never learned if he lived or died.

Strange Airplanes

On our work details we often heard what appeared to be airplanes. The sound came from above, but we couldn't determine what had made the sound. We thought the object making the noise must be very small. Finally, someone saw a plane ahead of the sound. We watched with awe as the plane flew by so fast. We could readily see that the American propeller planes were no match for this one.

These planes were the cause of much more concern than the propaganda about them. These were the first jet planes, but thankfully, they did not have sufficient fuel available to put them into combat operations.

Prisoners in the Barracks

The 180 men in our barracks were from most of the states. We ranged in age from 17 or 18 to the ripe old age of 28. Robert Riggs, a jeep driver, was from Fort Worth, Texas and only 22 years old. For some reason, he had false teeth. He was driving near the front line, apparently made the wrong turn and was surrounded by German soldiers. His teeth were in the glove compartment and he tried to get them. Apparently the captors thought he was trying to get a weapon. He would have been much less concerned if he had known how little he would need his teeth in prison.

A soldier from South Dakota had become shell shocked and wasn't responsible for his actions. He, like everyone else, was assigned to work details. Usually he would do whatever someone told him to do. Occasionally he would walk off and someone would tell the guard and lead him back. We found that by pointing a finger at our head, moving it in a circular motion and saying "spinning", the guard would understand. We usually told the guard beforehand. In camp, he laid on his bunk all the time. We were furnished cards to send to our families, and he would not complete the cards or give me the name and address of his family. He did know his name. I doubt his family heard from him while he was in the prison camp.

The cards we sent home were required to have the name and address of a family member so they could be mailed. We didn't question providing the requested information on these cards when we could send a message home. Oddly enough, this was the same information we refused to supply earlier, even when standing in front of a firing squad.

Our musician was Russell E. Banks from Elizabethtown, Kentucky. Someone found and brought to the barracks a musical instrument that appeared to be the relative of a guitar.

Russell soon learned to play it well and provided music for anyone to sing. If he didn't know the song, he would say, "sing it - I'll second", and he did well. He also told many stories about Kentucky. Some were about mountains so steep you could look up the chimney and see the cows coming home. The cows had two short legs on one side so they could walk around the mountains, and that you could ride a bicycle downhill anyway you wanted to go.

Every night he would sing one verse of an old ditty entitled, *"Somebody's Head's on the Pillow Where My Head's Suppose to Be".* He would sing one new verse every night, and no amount of persuasion or intimidation would ever discourage him from doing so. I felt sure he made up the new verse during every day.

A man from a tank outfit was also quite an entertainer and storyteller. He was from Morris, Alabama. He told stories about homemade alcohol that he made without a license.

There was only one Jewish fellow in the barracks and in his mind he got the worst of every situation. His job on the work detail was the most difficult, his potato was smaller, or his bowl of soup bowl not as full as someone else's. In his opinion, he was mistreated in every situation.

Two fellows who were good friends, at least in prison, had each served in another branch of the military. One had been in the Navy and the other in the Marines. The former Navy man would ask the Marine if the Marines were part of the Navy. The former Marine would counter by singing a little ditty, *"10,000 gobs laid down their swabs to fight one sick Marine. 10,000 stood up and swore it was the terriblest fight they had ever seen"*.

A fellow from Utah, and a Mormon, was some type of official in the Mormon Church. He did not qualify as a minister, so was required to work. He never quite resigned himself to having to do this.

People react differently in adverse conditions. Some complain and blame somebody or something for their situation. Some blamed the government, the officers, the non-corns, or just felt unlucky. Some complained about the food, the living conditions and some about the work details. Since I was the barracks leader, I heard all the stories.

I don't recall anyone mentioning their particular situation at the time they were captured by the Germans. If I had not been wearing my tape bandage, it's likely no one would have been aware of my injury. I don't recall telling anyone about the tank or hand grenade, or anyone telling me about their capture, except Robert Riggs, the jeep driver.

Some of the fellows had a pity party from day one. Others made the best of a bad situation and seemed upbeat about the whole affair. One fellow, who never complained, was an Indian from Eagle Butte, South Dakota, named Callus LeBlanc. Everyone seemed to feel better after talking to him.

Many strange things happened while we were on work details. Sometimes when the American or British bombers were dropping bombs, we would be taken to a bomb shelter. The shelters were made of concrete and were underground. Usually these shelters were reserved for the Germans. Generally, we would go to the basement of a large building. Sometimes we would sit under railroad cars. The railroad cars didn't protect us from the bombs, but they did protect us from the shrapnel fired by the Germans in an effort to down Allied planes.

On one occasion, we had been sent to the basement of a brewery. Bombs were landing nearby and the ground was shaking. A man entered the basement leading four large horses used to pull the beer wagon. He yelled at the guards to get us out, there was not enough room, he said. We were in a hallway about fifty yards long and ten or twelve feet wide. There was plenty of room, but he continued to complain to the guards, so we were taken outside and sat under a railroad car. We had been in the same basement many times before, and many times afterwards, but we never saw the man again.

One detail of eight or nine prisoners was taken to an official air raid shelter. Germans came to the shelter so the prisoners were sent to the railroad cars. After the air raid, the prisoners were sent back to help dig the people out. A bomb made a direct hit on the shelter.

Another group of prisoners was removing rubble from a damaged building when the roof collapsed, killing a soldier from Paris, Texas, and injuring W. T. Crawford from San Saba, Texas. W. T. Crawford limps to this day because of the injury.

I recall on one work site we saw 25 to 30 ill-clad men. They were chained together. Some of the men didn't have shoes, but had cloth and other material wrapped around their feet. I asked the guard who they were and he said, "political prisoners". I'm sure they were Jewish, but didn't know it at the time.

We continued to get our bowl of soup each day at noon. One day we had something different; they said it was mushroom soup. The taste was terrible. I gave my soup to another prisoner, who ate his own soup, as well as mine. Later that day he died.

The Piano

We were working on a street repair when a German civilian began talking to the guards. The civilian wasn't standing very close, and we didn't know what he wanted. He looked to be 25 to 30 years old, and one of the few men of that age we had seen who was not in uniform. He talked with the three guards, individually, and as a group.

Finally, one of the guards took four of us to go with the man. Some two blocks away we came to an apartment building that had received bomb damage. The stairwell area was destroyed. This man had placed a ladder to the second floor, which allowed entry through a large window. We climbed to the second floor, found some furniture, and a beautiful upright piano. The piano appeared to be his pride and joy, and he needed help in getting it to the ground.

The man and the guard discussed at length the proper procedure for lowering the piano. He had two small ropes that he felt were strong enough to hold the piano if we slid it down the ladder. The guard had other ideas. Sometimes they would yell at one another. We, the prisoners, found a place to sit.

Some thirty minutes into the conversation we sat the piano on the window ledge. The window was sufficiently large enough for the piano to pass through. Their conversation started again; we sat again. After tiring of listening to another lengthy conversation, we tied the ropes to the piano, sat it on the ladder, and easily slid it down to the ground. The man shook every prisoner's hand and thanked him personally. He didn't speak to the guard. I told the fellows that a meal would have been more appropriate.

I had the only watch and Bible (New Testament) in the barracks. We had Sunday devotionals and prayer. Many of the men borrowed my Bible and everyone wanted to know, "What time is it?" I often wondered how the crew ever knew when to be ready for work after I had already left.

Sunday's were the only non-work day, but they were also wash day. We washed as best we could in cold water without soap. We hung the clothes on the barbed wire fence. On the following Sunday, we washed our underwear. As soon as it was cold enough to freeze, we could hang the clothes out to freeze, and very soon bring them inside to finish drying. Usually, before Monday morning, everything was dry.

The weather continued to get colder, and we had only the clothes we wore when we were captured. It was cold enough in the barracks to freeze water most nights. I requested blankets and received them a day or two later. It seems there were not enough blankets, so they tore them in half. One-half of a blanket doesn't do very much good.

The only door to our barracks was on the north side. Snow began to build up on the small porch. I requested a snow shovel and one was delivered the same day. Before that, we had tried to keep the snow raked off the porch with our feet.

Despite the fact we had a coal-burning stove, we had no coal or anything to burn. On our work details, we would sometimes make a stack of wood from the damaged wood in the building and tie wire around it so we could carry it to the barracks. Some of the guards would let us take the wood through the front gate; others would make us leave it. We noted that the bundles were not by the gate the next morning, leading us to believe the guards used our wood for their own benefit.

Sometimes the guards would let us start a fire at work, especially if it was really cold. We would borrow matches or a cigarette lighter from the guard to start a fire. We would warm our feet and hands. The guards would not get their feet near the fire. If the issuing officer could smell smoke on the shoes, the soldiers would have to pay for the new shoes. If we could burn a few bundles of wood at night, the barracks would stay comfortable until morning. Troops from many countries were in the camp. Only three barracks were for Americans, the one immediately south of us and the barracks to the east, which was across the walkway.

Russian troops were in the barracks to the north of us. We didn't have anyone on either side to speak the other's language. We did hand signs and waved at them. The Russians did have small stoves with a hand cranked bellows. This would allow a person to cook something quickly and with very little fuel. Our problem was having something to cook. Once we traded something we found at work detail for the cooker.

The Russians didn't work on jobs like we did, but cut wood. One guard told us that the winter before, on a very cold day, the Russians refused to go to work. The Germans turned two German shepherd dogs loose in their barracks. The Russians were prepared with sticks with long nails through them. They soon killed and skinned the dogs. The guard didn't tell us what then happened to the dogs.

Christmas

The Germans celebrated Christmas even in the middle of war. We were not scheduled to work because of the holiday. Christmas day came and no breakfast. At noontime we received our first real meal since becoming prisoners. We were served mashed potatoes with seasoning, two slices of rye bread, a piece of meat that I could not identify, and a piece of cake. We hoped this would mean more food in the future.

After noon we were allowed to go to a larger building, along with the men of the other barracks. Russell Banks took his 5-string instrument and supplied the music. We did the proper thing by having prayer first. Some of the men who could sing well sang Christmas songs, and others led the group in singing. Not everyone opted to come, but I think more than 500, of the 540 total prisoners-of-war, attended.

After returning to our barracks, we were informed that beer was available. In reality there were only two kegs for three barracks. I wondered how you could divide the beer equally for the 180 soldiers.

We met in the walkway between the barracks, so everyone could come to the fence to see what happened. A guard gave each of the barracks' leaders an aluminum coin; the odd man didn't get a keg. I hoped it would be me so as to eliminate the hassle, and the fact that I didn't drink. We flipped the coins, mine was the odd one. I was really happy.

Back at the barracks, the men were almost in tears. Some

complained like little kids. I agreed to resign as barracks' leader, but they didn't want that. Later that evening, we were given our boiled potato and slice of black bread. The following day, another non-work day, noon came and no food. I asked and was informed that we had a double portion of food the previous day. The men complained more about not getting the beer than not getting food. The food was horrible, not enough to eat, and for the first two or three weeks, the hunger pains were very difficult to deal with. Later we either became accustomed to the hunger pains, or they just didn't bother us so much.

The guards seemed to have sufficient food, and we noted they were smoking American cigarettes. We suspected they were getting food parcels intended for the prisoners. On several occasions I asked the Camp Commander about the food parcels but was told none were received at that camp. During my time as a prisoner, we only received food parcels one time, and they were shared with other prisoners.

The German People

I was amazed that the German people were not more resentful toward the Americans. After all, most of the bomb damage came from the Americans. We knew Munich was hit every day, especially at night. Sometimes we would work side by side with civilians and they didn't show resentment.

Even in wartime, the streets were swept, the windows washed and trash removed. They were a neat and orderly people.

Early in the week when I was to go on the farm detail, I ate something (cabbage soup) which upset my stomach. I was outside the barracks and my head became very dizzy. When I awoke I was on my bunk and the fellows acted as if nothing had happened. The next morning I seemed to be fine and went to work as usual. I did wonder if the lack of food and loss of weight might have been a factor.

Everything was rationed; we sometimes found ration books in the damaged buildings. It took cash, which we didn't have, and someone to buy items for you.

The German people looked well fed and clothed. Most wore uniforms of some type. We noticed they didn't say "Good Morning" when they met, but said, "Heil Hitler".

On Thursday during the first week of March, 1945, a list of twenty names was sent to each of the three barracks of Americans. Those listed were to go on a farm detail on the following Saturday. My name and five other names were from our barracks, the remaining names were from the other two barracks.

The following day, Friday, two prisoners were left in camp to help unload a railroad car of the terrible black bread. The two of us arrived at the railroad area of camp before the railroad car was unlocked. A German soldier was driving a tractor of sorts, pulling a flatbed trailer. It was cold that morning, so we walked up behind the tractor to get some heat from the tractor exhaust. The driver turned around and spoke to us in perfect English. Most of the right side of his face, including his right eye, was missing. He informed us he was wounded on the Russian front. He also said his parents had moved from Germany to Chicago some years before the war. His parents felt Germany would win the war, so they sent their son to join the German military. He said when the war was over, he would get a brown uniform (American), and go home with the rest of us. The railroad car was opened; we started to work and didn't get to talk to him again.

Farm Detail

We were to leave on Saturday at 8:00 a.m. It was not difficult to pack; we simply put our clothes on and walked out of the barracks. I did give my small Russian cooker to a fellow prisoner. I didn't arrange to have someone else elected as barracks leader.

We were issued three cans of food with a hole punched in the top to prevent our saving food for an escape attempt. I had my paratrooper pants with large pockets and could carry the cans easily. The contents were not liquid and did not leak. The others needed a sack or box, but none was furnished. Each of us had a small folding can opener issued by the U.S. Army.

We rode the open boxcar to Munich, walked a mile or more to another railroad station. We went to the lobby area where both civilian and military personnel were waiting. We stood in a group with the three guards. When the train was announced, we went aboard with everyone else. A guard stood at each end of the car. We were told to sit in any empty seat. I sat by a man who had some family members living in Kansas. He wanted to talk to someone from Kansas. The five others from our barracks were not from Kansas, and I didn't know about the remaining fourteen.

In less than an hour we were in a railroad yard and the air raid siren was sounding. Everyone else left along with one of our guards. He soon returned and led us to the basement of a large house. The guard said the house belonged to Herman Goering. The City was Rosenheim. Soon the all clear sounded and we boarded the train again. We continued south again for another ten or fifteen minutes. The train stopped; we got off and waited for the train to pass. We then headed east up a steep gravel road. After walking about one and one-half miles, we came to a small town. The sign said Nussdorf. On the right was a small stone building with a barbed wire fence around the front of the building. One guard was waiting for us.

Nußdorf/Inn mit Heuberg

The three guards that brought us walked back down the road toward the railroad tracks. We examined the building and found twenty bunks, without the hay mattresses. There was running water, a flush toilet and a shower without hot water.

The guard was outside, so we had a discussion about escape. We realized we would have more freedom. We were not in good health, I had lost about sixty pounds, and the other prisoners had lost like amounts. There was snow in the ditches by the road and the weather was still pretty cold. We agreed to build up our strength and try to escape later. We felt the war would end soon.

I think we all opened a can of food and ate part of it. This food was to feed us until Monday morning when we were to work for a family. One of the men in our group spoke fluent German, and most of us could understand some German and speak a little.

The building had no windows and only one door. This door opened on the front and inside the barbed wire enclosure. We found the back portion of the fence was not completed and we could walk in and out. There was a gate with a lock. After the noon hour, a short heavyset man came in with the guard. He was the Mayor and would take each of us to the family assigned. He took one man at a time to a farm, except two men were assigned to a larger farm.

Most of the twenty men had been assigned before he reached my name. The Mayor didn't seem to have the benefit of a bath for some length of time. We walked two or three blocks to a large white three-story house. He called loudly and a large woman came to the balcony on the second floor. The Mayor introduced me to Frau Moser. Soon a girl of 18 or 19 came out on the balcony with a hay mattress for me. Frau Moser told me that someone would get me at 7:00 a.m. on Monday.

The guard had served on the Russian front and his nose had been frozen. His nose was rather large and red. Someone nicknamed him "cherry nose". He didn't know the meaning, but didn't object. We took turns washing clothes Saturday afternoon, Saturday night and Sunday. We had to dry them inside since the building was near the street. We did take wet clothes for others and hang them on the fence to dry.

The guard carried on a conversation with someone all the time, especially the man who spoke German well. He left his rifle and walked off; someone hid it under a hay mattress. We checked and the rifle was not loaded. We returned the rifle but knew there wasn't much security. We had more food than we were accustomed to both Saturday and Sunday. Some of the fellows saved some of the food in case the farmers didn't feed us well.

On Monday morning at 7:00 a.m., a boy of 11 or 12 was at the gate to pick me up. He held my hand for the two blocks to the house. When we arrived, Frau Moser introduced me to the family. The girl I met was Agathe, age 19, a younger girl, 15, named Theresa, who they called Risa, and Frau Moser's mother, who was probably 65 or 70. Lastly, she took me to the master bedroom where I met the farmer, Herr Moser. He had suffered a stroke, which badly affected his face, right arm and right side to some extent. He couldn't talk clearly, not even the family could understand him. Mrs. Moser fed him in the bedroom. We then went to the kitchen, which contained a dining room table, a wood burning cookstove, cabinets and countertop around the room, except behind the stove.

We stood around the table and they said grace in unison, the Catholic version, "Hail Mary full of grace". Then we sat around the table, except Grandmother, who sat by the stove. Apparently I had taken her place at the table. We had fresh sliced wheat bread; the bread was sliced at the table by hand, along with butter and jelly. I knew it wouldn't be all bad if I had sufficient food to eat. I thought about the hard work I had done on the farm where I was raised. After breakfast we walked down the hall toward the back of the house to a doorway. Inside that door were twelve milk cows and two oxen. The cows were lying on leaves and had a chain around their neck to keep them in place. There was very little odor and I didn't smell them in the house.

The girls and grandmother hitched the oxen to a farm wagon. Grandmother and I got on the wagon, she talked to the oxen and off we went. There were no lines or ropes to control the oxen, like on the teams of horses at home. We headed for the mountains not far away. When we reached an area of trees we stopped. Grandmother pitched some nets off the wagon. The nets were eight to ten feet square with a stick eight or ten inches tall tied to one corner. There were two leaf rakes, so we started raking leaves in piles. I had seen the cows lying on leaves, so I knew the reason to get more. We placed the leaves in the nets and passed the small stick through the net material to form a ball. We had several balls ready when she retrieved a picnic basket out of the wagon. She said, "Brotzeit", which meant we would stop and eat. The food was more of the good bread and jelly.

We finished loading the wagon with the leaves in the nets. The wagon was piled high. We returned to the house, and on the way I recall thinking that they were not concerned about my leaving, since I could have easily left on this trip. After unloading the leaves, stacking them in a corner of the barn, and taking the harness off the oxen and placing them in the barn, I was told to sit on a bench by the barn door.

In a few minutes Frau Moser introduced me to the man next door who spoke English, as well as six other languages. He was an artist and writer. He was married and had a son 6 or 7 years old named Adrain. He also had two sons in the army from a previous marriage. He told me the Moser's couldn't pronounce either my first or last name. He thought I might have a nickname. I told him I didn't have one. He did establish that I was from Texas, so he told the family to call me "Tex". He said it was lunchtime; he would go home, but after lunch, he would come back to talk some more. We ate lunch, potato salad and bread. The neighbor returned and we sat in the house and talked most of the afternoon.

The house was three stories. The first floor consisted of a living room and one bedroom on one side of the hall; the other side was the master bedroom and the kitchen/dining combination. At the end of the hall was a stairway to the second floor. There were three bedrooms on each side of the hall. Another stairway went to the third floor where there were four bedrooms. People whose homes had been bombed or burned were assigned by the government to live there. The tenants were an elderly couple; the man was not able to walk up the stairs. I only saw the woman when she went to the store. A widow had the responsibility of a girl who was 13 or 14 and her brother, Eric, who had led me from the barracks. The lady prepared food for the three of them; they were not her family.

More of the building was for the barn than the house. There was a full basement with only one room for household use. The remainder was storage for waste from the cattle.

We ate again, the evening meal, a potato soup that was rather good. I then left alone for the barracks. I was the first to return. As the others came in, they told of the hard work they had done. None of the men except me ate with the family. Some of the men had not been allowed in the house. That was not surprising since we were enemy prisoners. We realized that we could leave, but we were unarmed, except for "Cherry Nose's" rifle, minus ammunition. We agreed to wait and see what would happen.

I continued to eat with the family, which also consisted of a boy 17, Peter Junior, who had been injured in the German Army and discharged. Even though he was not in the service, he was required to ride a bicycle several miles each way to work in a government factory. He was very friendly and likeable, but got home late each day.

Apparently, some person in authority heard that I was eating with the family and came by to correct the situation. Mrs. Moser told him "those who worked hard must eat well". I was unaware of the inquiry, and continued to eat meals with the family.

The two girls and I worked at times on the land they farmed. We plowed some of the land, ran a harrow over sections, picked up rocks, and hauled barnyard fertilizer. The oxen, named Murik and Mox, were the source of power.

The town of Nussdorf was quite unique. A stream ran through town, through a concrete ditch, which was two meters deep and two meters wide. Five water wheels operated from the water, two generating electricity, two flour mills, and one saw mill. The generators provided electricity for the entire village. I estimated the population to be about 200, consisting basically of farmers whose houses had been built in a cluster for protection. The Moser's house had been built in 1812. A Moser several generations back had bought the land and tore the existing house down before building the present house. Most houses were very old, one dating to 1631.

The people in the town were friendly. Many of them came by to see what an American looked like. The neighbor who spoke English came by every day and sometimes more often. He told me he needed to practice his English. He also said that Mr. Moser had not been a supporter of Hitler, and some years before had predicted that Germany would lose the war. Mr. Moser had a stroke before the authorities came to see him, otherwise he would have been in prison.

He gave me some local history. The town of Nussdorf was rather new for Germany, being only 600 years old. Originally, it was a natural lake, but for some reason the dam broke. Gradually farmers moved in, built their houses in a cluster and farmed the land. The stream of water coming through town was man-made about 100 years before. A water gate was put in the Inn River at a higher altitude, causing the rapid flow downhill.

The streets were maintained by conscripted labor from the townspeople. They were graveled and the town owned a rock crusher. Some of the other prisoners were sent to work on the streets for one day only; I didn't have to go on that work duty.

One day they asked me to haul barnyard fertilizer to a field on the west side of town. By now I could harness the oxen and speak well enough to drive them. After loading the wagon, I began the journey of about a mile. The land was adjacent to the road. By passing the land for 300 to 400 yards, you could cross a bridge and return on the other side of the bar ditch. I decided to cross the bar ditch which was 30 or 40 feet wide. It didn't look bad, even though a small amount of snow was still visible. I commanded the oxen to turn right, and as they entered the ditch area, they sank to their bellies. I didn't know the word for backing up, so I continued urging the oxen on. When the wagon reached the ditch, it sank to the wagon bed and was pushing some six inches of mud. The oxen kept pulling and gradually pulled the wagon back on high ground. Both the oxen and wagon were muddy. I unloaded the fertilizer and returned by the bridge. When I arrived at the house, Herr Moser was standing outside with his cane. He pushed some mud off the front of the wagon with the cane and I think he tried to laugh. No one mentioned it to me.

The two girls milked the twelve cows. The milk was put in large cans. The cans were put on a little hand-pulled wagon with wheels built like a farm wagon. The boy, Eric, usually pulled the wagon to a designated place about two blocks away. After the milk had been picked up and empty cans left, he would go and get the wagon and empty cans. One day one of the back wheels was broken when he returned. When Peter returned from the factory, Frau Moser asked him to repair the wheel which needed a new hub, a wooden part about six inches in diameter and six inches long. He started by locating a square block of wood and cutting off the desired length with a band saw. With hand tools, he fashioned the hub to fit the axle and proper holes to accommodate the spokes. He finished the task in an hour or so, a task that I couldn't have done in a week.

A neighbor had a son who was in the army and was badly injured. After hospital care, he was allowed to remain at home to recuperate. We traded war stories, and he would come over on his crutches to pass the time of day. His injury came from an artillery shell that destroyed a house and killed most of his companions. An officer had been killed and was lying across his leg. He could not move the man or remove his leg. He told me he had to cut the officer's leg off so he could get out. As time went by, German troops, each with a rifle, came through town heading for the mountains. Everyone knew the war was just about over. Every day or two, I would tune the radio to BBC to hear a news report. The family would go to some other part of the house, so they wouldn't know I was changing the station. The authorities would let people listen to only one radio station for fear they would hear some propaganda.

Every two weeks or so, a woman in uniform came by to weigh the milk from each cow. She also tried to count the chickens, but wasn't very successful at doing that. She did allow Mr. Moser to have an egg each morning. We continued working in the fields and even planted potatoes in April. I found they planted the whole potato, while at home we planted potatoes that were cut into several pieces, each with an "eye". I tried to explain, but they felt the cut potatoes would rot. Finally, they agreed to plant two short rows after I had cut them into "eye" pieces.

On the morning of April 12, possibly April 13, "Cherry Nose" came in the barracks and informed us that Roosevelt had died. He was sure America would stop fighting and Germany would then win the war. We, the prisoners, could not think of the name of the Vice President. I did recall he was formerly a Senator from Missouri. It was after I arrived at work and listened to the radio that I found out the Vice President was Harry Truman. If the Moser's knew about Roosevelt's death, they didn't mention it, nor did the English speaking neighbor.

During my time as a prisoner, I had not seen a civilian automobile, only a few trucks. In Munich a great number of horses and wagons were used for delivery. Trains were used exclusively for long distance hauling and traveling. More and more German troops were coming through town. Mrs. Moser treated me like one of the children. She was concerned that some German soldier would shoot me on my way to and from the barracks.

Mrs. Moser and the neighbor told me that many of the soldiers had been on the front against the Russian Army, but came to this area to be captured by the Americans. I saw Peter talking to several of them, but he didn't talk to me about them. At the barracks we stayed inside as much as possible, since the road was only a few feet from our fence. Mrs. Moser arranged for a girl, who was 8 or 9, to walk with me on my returning in the afternoon to the barracks. Usually she held my hand; I'm sure Mrs. Moser suggested it.

On April 30, 1945, I started walking to work from the barracks. I left before the others, since I ate breakfast with the Moser's. About a block from the barracks as I was nearing an intersection of streets, I saw three large black cars approaching. The cars turned at the corner, a few feet from where I was standing. The first car had five or six guards, each holding a rifle. My first concern was that I would be shot, but none of the guards even glanced my way. The second car had two guards, also holding rifles. In the back of the second car in a glassed enclosure sat Adolph Hitler. He was looking directly at me. He looked old and tired. Although he was only 56 years old, he looked much older. The third car had guards like the first vehicle. I stood and waited for some of my fellow prisoners to come by so I could tell them about Hitler. While I waited, I saw three small airplanes, piper cub-type, leave from 300 to 400 yards away. I could not tell who was aboard two of the planes, but I know the passenger in the middle plane was Adolph Hitler. After all the guards had passed, each with the SS insignia, I could understand Mrs. Moser's concern for my safety.

From everything I have read, Hitler was out of his mind and unable to make proper decisions. At the time I saw him, no one was with him except the guards. Someone may have been in command who rode in one of the three airplanes. The planes were so small that no more than one person in addition to the pilot could have ridden in each plane. None of the fellows appeared while this occurred and it was time for breakfast. I walked on to the Moser's home. When I arrived, they all told me at once that Hitler had spent the night with Mr. Pullen, the rich man on the hill. Peter told me that Mr. Pullen addressed Hitler as "Adolph" while everyone else called him "Mein Fuhrer".

Peter was not going to work because the war was all but over. We looked outside and saw hundreds of German troops standing and sitting around. Mrs. Moser asked me not to leave the house. Peter had been out, came back and told us that the Mayor's daughter had carried a jug of milk under her fur coat up to the house for Hitler. He was having stomach problems and milk was all he could have.

Everybody who came by talked about Hitler. All of them expected someone to announce the surrender. The man next door came over and talked about Hitler. He assured me that the man spending the night of April 29, 1945, was the real Hitler and not a "look-alike".

During the day, many American fighter planes flew over rather low. I didn't hear any shots from all the German soldiers in the area. I did listen to BBC, which predicted the war would end on May 1st. After the evening meal, Mrs. Moser told me not to go back to the barracks, but to spend the night with them. A German officer came in and asked to listen to the radio to get information for the troops. He didn't stay long. I wondered if he was concerned that he was outside and I was in the warm house. Bedtime came and I slept in a double bed with Peter. It was a feather bed, very soft and comfortable. I wondered if "Cherry Nose" had been notified that I wasn't going to return to the barracks, or if anyone really cared. I thought about the old statement, "War certainly makes strange bed fellows".

The following day we did nothing but look out the window at hundreds more defeated German soldiers. You could see defeat in their eyes, the way they walked, and the way they looked. I didn't see any of them eating, though they likely had something equivalent to our K-Rations. I listened to the radio every few hours, but the Moser's never turned it on. That night it snowed about six inches. By noon most of the snow had melted, at least where the sun had shined on it.

I spent another night in Peter's wonderful bed. By 9:00 a.m. on May 2nd, 1945, I heard someone speaking German over a loud speaker, asking the troops to stack their rifles and board the army buses (school bus-type). The rifles were stacked neatly in perfect rows. The previous day I had seen a German General go into a building across the street. He went to the second floor and into a room.

After shaking hands with Herr Moser and Peter, I hugged Frau Moser and the girls. They all cried and seemed sorry I was leaving. I crossed the street, went to the second floor, and knocked on the door. The General came to the door and handed me his sword as a token of surrender. He then went downstairs and walked over to join the soldiers getting on the buses.

Only four American soldiers with one jeep and one half-track from the Second Armored Division came to Nussdorf, where hundreds of German soldiers had surrendered. I didn't know it at the time, but Peter had gone to the church, removed the German flag, and hung a white flag of surrender. In addition to the buses, there were five small automobiles belonging to high-ranking officers. I took the first automobile, along with three of my fellow prisoners. The jeep, half-track, and small automobiles worked out well in that all twenty American prisoners could ride comfortably.

We followed the buses, which were driven by the Germans, who were following the jeep and half-track. There was not much gas in any of the cars. They were probably Volkswagen's with four forward speeds. We went to a small town some twenty miles from Nussdorf. The Sergeant who spoke to the German troops went in a house and loudly informed the occupants to leave. Some eight or ten people, including a young lady with a small baby, lived there. We didn't see them again except for the young mother, who came back the following day and knocked very lightly on the side door. She asked if she could get some clothes for the baby.

I told her to take what she wanted.

The twenty of us ate everything we could find in the house within the first thirty minutes. No military people were there except two tanks. They said they had no food, but did offer to loan us a skillet and seasoning if we found something to cook. I noticed that next door there were chickens in a fenced yard, so I knocked on the door and asked for some eggs. The lady had fourteen; I had some coins I had picked up. She selected the proper amount from my hand. With the skillet, butter substitute, pepper and salt, we had scrambled eggs. Only eight of us were there at the time. We cooked outside on the small stove from the tankers, but ate on plates from the house. The fourteen eggs weren't a big meal for the eight of us.

Soon the others returned, saw that we had cooked eggs, and one buddy asked me to get more eggs. I suggested that he get eggs for himself. He said he didn't know how to ask for them. I had him practice a few times and he went nearby, knocked on the door and asked for eggs. The lady replied "nein" (meaning no in German). The soldiers said, "I'll take them".

Our departure plane was to fly in about 3:00 p.m., but it began to rain and rained for two days. The plane was to land on a mat landing strip so we had to wait. We drove around for some time in the car, but the gas was very low. I saw a truck with gasoline in five gallon cans. I spoke with the driver, and he gave me one can. We drove around more and came upon an army bakery in a trailer truck. The Sergeant gave each of us a loaf of bread (one pound size). It was not sliced but was still warm. I still remember that bread as being delicious.

We decided to return to Nussdorf where we felt we could get food to eat. On the way, someone was shooting at us; finally hit a fender of the car, so we turned back around. After getting back to the town, we found that a small store had opened. He had bread, butter and some liverwurst. We lived on this until the DC3 came two days later and took us to Rheims, France.

We first showered and donned new clothes in France; our old clothes were destroyed. I had received a barracks bag to put all my personal equipment for safe-keeping. I had the sword from the German General, my knife, watch, pocket Bible and my billfold. When I finished showering, my sword was gone. I hated to lose the one memento I had secured. We were issued a meal ticket. This ticket had to be punched every time we were in a food line. We spent long hours in food lines, but we had nothing else to do.

On May 8th we were informed that the Germans were coming to surrender. General Eisenhower's headquarters were across the road from the camp. It was a French schoolhouse. The press referred to it as the "Little Red Schoolhouse". We sat on the ground across the road and sure enough, here came a jeep-looking vehicle with a driver and a naval officer. The officer went inside for about 45 minutes. He returned to his vehicle and they drove off toward Germany.

In the food line that afternoon I heard someone calling my name. I turned toward the sound and didn't see anyone I knew. Then a fellow I graduated from high school with stepped from behind someone else. His name was Ernest Mack Boyd. He had also been a POW.

We were given a glass of eggnog each night. We were not supposed to eat too much. I felt I had been eating well for about three months and the extra food wouldn't hurt me.

A few days later we caught a passenger train to Le Havre and Camp Lucky Strike, a port for all types of personnel headed toward the States. The first day there I met Ben Day, another 1940 graduate from Sulphur Springs High. He had been shot down over Sicily and had been a prisoner for a long time. He had received mail from home. His mother had told him that Joe Craver, a 1939 high school graduate, had been captured. His wife had a baby and if I saw him, to be sure and tell him. A few minutes later I met Joe, informed him that he had a baby. His first question, "is it a boy or girl?" I admitted I hadn't asked. He went home without knowing.

One afternoon we loaded on a small ship, "U.S.S. Sea Owl", a wartime ship made by the Kaiser Company. We went to sleep in Le Havre, the next morning we were in London harbor. A number of hospital patients were loaded on the ship in the afternoon, we headed for the open seas, heading home.

We traveled alone; the trip was uneventful. The small ship was rather rough in the Atlantic and several of the fellows were seasick. The rest of us would clean up and go to the galley for soup and crackers. When we were about three days out from Boston, we ran into a squall, navy talk, it was quite a storm. The ship turned into the wind, and we were told three days later that we were still in the same place. In the meantime, all but ten or twelve of us were in the bunks seasick. It took a lot of cleaning and many trips to the galley, but in three days we docked in Boston, Pier 16. This was the same pier I had departed from.

We off-loaded, boarded a train and rode a few miles to an army camp. We were served a steak dinner. German prisoners-of-war were serving, and we had been warned not to even speak to them. Afterwards we reloaded on the train and headed for San Antonio, Texas.

After the War

Because the Mosers had been good to me, we sent a few care packages to the family. We exchanged Christmas cards for two or three years. Since neither of us could read nor write the other's language, we stopped sending cards to each other.

In September, 1983, my wife, Sarah, and I went to Europe with our youngest daughter, Diane Garland. We rented a car in Frankfurt and toured part of Germany. When we were near Nussdorf, we drove by to see if we could find the Moser's house. The town had grown so that I had a difficult time locating the house. No one answered the bell at the Moser's home. But I saw a young lady looking out of the door of an apartment which had been built behind the Moser's house.

This was the residence of Peter's oldest son, and the young lady could speak English. She informed me that Peter, the Assistant Mayor, was in France at the "Sister City". Agate, the oldest daughter, lived across town. She led us to her house where Agate recognized me and hugged my neck.

After visiting with Agate for a short time, she prepared some fine food and insisted we spend the night with her and her husband, Wolfgang Dettendorfer. They own and operate a dairy of about 100 cows.

We were informed that Mr. Moser and Mrs. Moser's mother had died soon after the war. Mrs. Moser had died in 1975. Peter had sold the cows and made the barn into part of the house. He also built a larger building behind the house for his woodworking business where he employs 20 to 25 people.

We left for Austria and Switzerland and told them we would be back in a week. When we returned, they had rolled out the "red carpet". We ate and visited and finally an English-speaking newspaper reporter came by for a story for the local paper.

We enjoyed the time together, the old house, and the tour of the quaint little village on the slope of the Alps. .

In 1985 our oldest daughter, Becky, and her husband, Leslie Flanery, went to Europe with Sarah and me. While there, we went by the Moser's home and had a great time. On this trip Peter informed me that everyone now cuts their potatoes before planting, due to my suggestion in 1945. One day we drove some 40 miles to the small town where Theresa lives. She is the youngest daughter of the Moser's.

In 1989 our two middle daughters, Linda Robinson and Annette Williams, went with me to Europe. Sarah had planned to go, but her knee was causing pain, so she decided not to make the trip. All four of my girls have now been to the Moser's home, which probably means more to me than it does to them. I also had plans to interview Peter and several other folks in

Nussdorf about the time Hitler stayed there, so I would have some additional supportive information for my memoires.

Annette, Linda and I had a good time, saw much of the country and visited the Moser family again. We tried to get some recorded statements about Hitler being in Nussdorf April 29 and April 30, 1945, but the local Chief of Police, who was also in attendance, cut short the meeting we had set up with several local folks for that purpose. As soon as Annette turned on the recorder and I asked the first question, the Chief turned to Peter Moser and suggested in German that we all go to a restaurant and have Streusel – end of interview.

Before I was released as a prisoner-of-war I had written a letter, "To Whom it May Concern", telling them how well I had been treated by the Moser's. After the Americans were in command, a soldier came by and took the Moser's radio. The Moser's showed the soldier the letter I had written and he returned the radio to them.

The cards we were allowed to send home had five lines, each line about four inches long. Nothing could be written between the lines or past the margin. I sent most cards to my wife, but some were sent to my parents.

One of those addressed to my parents was read over a German

shortwave broadcast. Some fifty or more people wrote to my parents and told them of the broadcast. Most of the letters my parents received were from the East Coast where the shortwave radio reception was better. My folks also received a telegram from the War Department in Washington. My Mother and Dad kept all the letters and correspondence, which I now have in my possession. My Mother wrote letters of thanks to all who supplied a return address on their correspondence. The broadcast was heard on March 23, 1945.

There was an empty building across a narrow street from the Moser's house. In March, 1945, a long antenna was placed by the building and insulation placed on the inside. Peter was told that shortwave broadcasts were to be made. The reason was to send propaganda overseas. I often wondered if the broadcast was made across the street from my workplace in Nussdorf.

My back was damaged quite badly due to the injury sustained while in the foxhole, and I was in pain all of the time. If I did something to irritate my back, the pain was much more severe. It wasn't until 1973 that the pain ceased after a healing in our church.

In concluding, I've often wondered why no-one paid attention to the fact that I saw Hitler the same day he was supposed to have committed suicide in Berlin. Hitler was evil, truly evil, but he wasn't stupid. I realize that he had doubles stand in for him during the war, but the war was over and the man I saw was him, not a double. Personally, I believe Hitler did have a "look-alike" stationed in Berlin, who supposedly committed suicide. But the Hitler I saw on the morning of April 30, 1945, was the real deal, the man who spent the night of April 29, 1945, in Nussdorf, before leaving the next day for Argentina, Brazil, or some other place where he lived out his life. Who's to say otherwise, because the stated facts of his death as we know them don't support whatever really happened to him. Even the Russians, who in 1945 believed they had recovered a portion of his skull, found out in 2009 through DNA testing, that it really belonged to a woman, less than 40 years old. Wouldn't it be nice to know the truth?

4.

AFFIDAVIT OF AUBREY M. TEMPLES

State of Texas

County of Dallas

The undersigned Aubrey M. Temples, being duly sworn, hereby deposes and says:

1. I am over the age of 18 and a resident of the state of Texas. I have personal knowledge of the facts stated herein, and if called as a witness could testify completely thereto.

2. I suffer no legal disabilities and have personal knowledge of the facts set forth below.

"On November 1, 1943, I was inducted into the U.S. Army at the age of nineteen (19) at the Tyler, Texas induction station. After training and transport to England, I and others were assigned to the 82nd Airborne Division as regular paratrooper replacements. We were to jump in Holland in September, 1944 with the objective of destroying a German ammunition dump just outside the small town of Mook, Holland. The jump actually occurred on September 17, 1944. We found and destroyed the ammunition dump by firing into it so that it destroyed itself.

Several weeks later, while still on the front lines, our company was overrun by German tanks. An explosion occurred in the foxhole I shared with John Martin. I was removed from the foxhole by Germans and taken prisoner. I had suffered significant rib, shoulder and back injuries. I was interrogated along with other U.S. soldiers that had been captured on several occasions and moved between several German army camps over a period of time. Eventually, a small group of us were taken to the small German town of Nussdorf, a municipality in the district of Rosenheim in the state of Bavaria in Germany, not far from the Austrian border. We were assigned to work for specific German families in the town. I was assigned to work for the Moser family who ran a small dairy farm with twelve cows.

At this late stage in the war, our guards were rather lax on security and we thought about escaping. However, snow was still on the ground and we were still rather weak from malnourishment during our months of being held. We also felt the war would end soon. I became quite close to the family to which I was assigned and was even allowed to eat meals with them. Mr. and Mrs. Moser had three children, a 19 year old girl Agathe, a 17 year old boy named Peter and a 15 year old girl Theresa (called Risa).

On April 30, 1945, I started walking to work from the barracks. I left before my fellow prisoners of war, since I ate breakfast with the Mosers. About a block from the barracks as I was nearing an intersection of streets, I saw three large black cars approaching. The cars turned at the corner, a few feet from where I was standing and stopped. The first car had five or six guards,

-1-

75

each holding a rifle. I was wearing my 82nd Airborne uniform, so they knew I was a prisoner. My first concern was that I would be shot, but none of the guards even glanced my way. I'm assuming now that they did not shoot me because they were ordered to keep quiet. No one else was on the streets.

The second car had two guards, also holding rifles. It stopped right in front of me. In the back of the second car in a glassed enclosure sat Adolph Hitler. He was looking directly at me. He looked old and tired. Although he was only 56 years old, he looked much older. The third car had guards like the first vehicle. The cars then proceeded to the edge of town and stopped near an open field.

I stood and waited for some of my fellow prisoners to come by so I could tell them about seeing Hitler. While I waited, I saw and heard the running engines of three small airplanes (piper cub-type with extra large wheels for landing and taking off in unpaved areas). The people in the cars got out. Some of them including Hitler walked up the hill about 30 yards to the planes and boarded. A couple of them were younger men in civilian clothes. The guards had to help Hitler get in his plane. They took off from 300 to 400 yards away. Those left on the ground got back into the cars and drove off. Neither Eva Braun, nor Hitler's dog were with him. None of my fellow prisoners appeared while this was occurring and it was time for breakfast. I walked on to the Moser's home.

When I arrived, they all told me at once that Hitler had spent the night with Mr. Pullen, a wealthy resident of Nussdorf who lived on a nearby hill. Peter had been out, but when he came back, he told me that Mr. Pullen addressed Hitler as "Adolph" while everyone else called him "Mein Fuhrer". He also said that the Mayor's daughter had carried a jug of milk under her fur coat up to the house for Hitler. He was having stomach problems and milk was all he could have.

Later, we looked outside and saw hundreds of German troops standing and sitting around. Mrs. Moser asked me not to leave the house. Everybody who came by talked about Hitler having been there. The man next door came over and talked about it too. He assured me that the man spending the night of April 29, 1945, was the real Hitler and not a "look-alike".

During the day many American fighter planes flew over rather low. I didn't hear any shots from all the German soldiers in the area. I did listen to the BBC, which predicted the war would end on May 1st. After the evening meal, Mrs. Moser told me not to go back to the barracks, but to spend the night with them. A German officer came in and asked to listen to the radio to get information for the troops. He didn't stay long.

The following day we did nothing but look out the window at hundreds more defeated German soldiers. You could see defeat in their eyes, the way they walked, and the way they looked.

-2-

At 9 AM on May 2nd, 1945, I heard someone speaking German over a loud speaker, asking the troops to stack their rifles and board the army buses. Only four American soldiers with one jeep and one half-track from the Second Armored Division came to Nussdorf, where hundreds of German solders had surrendered. In addition to the buses, there were five small automobiles belonging to high-ranking officers. I took the first automobile, along with three of my fellow prisoners and we started our trip home. We flew out on a DC3 to Rheims, France. A few days later we caught a passenger train to Le Havre and then loaded onto a small ship the U.S.S. Sea Owl and headed back to the U.S."

I declare to the best of my knowledge and belief, the information herein is true, correct and complete.

Executed this the _2.1_ day of _January_, 20_15_.

Aubrey M. Temples
Signature of Aubrey M. Temples

NOTARY ACKNOWLEDGMENT

State of _Texas_, County of _Dallas_.

This instrument was acknowledged before me on the _21_ day of _January_, 20_15_ by Aubrey M. Temples, author of the above statement and he is known by me to be the person represented. In addition, the two persons signing below also witnessed the signing of the above affidavit by Aubrey M. Temples.

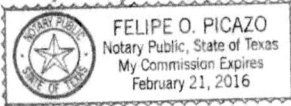

FELIPE O. PICAZO
Notary Public, State of Texas
My Commission Expires
February 21, 2016

Felipe Picazo
Notary Public in and for
the state of _Texas_

Felipe Picazo
Printed Name of Notary

(Notary Seal)

My Commission Expires:

_2|21|16_

SIGNATURE WITNESSES

Annabelle B. Hancock   _GEORGE B. OWEN_
Printed Name of Witness   Printed Name of Witness

Annabelle B. Hancock   _George B. Owen_
Witness Signature   Witness Signature

-3-

Return:

LEWIS ROBINSON
1006 POPOISE ST
LAKEWAY TX 78734

FILED AND RECORDED
OFFICIAL PUBLIC RECORDS

Dana DeBeauvoir

Jan 23, 2015 04:20 PM   2015010956
CLINTONB: $38.00
Dana DeBeauvoir, County Clerk
Travis County TEXAS